A VERY
SHORT
BOOK
ABOUT
WRITING

Darling Alice

with love

♡

Jonathan X

First published in 2021
by the Black Spring Press Group
Grantully Road, Maida Vale, London W9,
United Kingdom
This imprint: Eyewear

Cover design and typeset by Edwin Smet
Author photograph Arved Colvin-Smith

The right of Jonathan Davies to be identified as author of
this work has been asserted in accordance with section 77
of the Copyright, Designs and Patents Act 1988

Editor's note:
the typography has been selected by the author.

ISBN 978-1-913606-67-1

THE **BLACK SPRING**
PRESS GROUP

BLACKSPRINGPRESSGROUP.COM

A VERY SHORT BOOK ABOUT WRITING

JONATHAN G DAVIES

For
Amy, Sonali and Will

CONTENTS

INTRODUCTION

I have always wanted to write. Something. The urge has been there for most of my life. As long as I can remember. Books and words have moved me, inspired me and I've long had a feeling there is a novel inside me. Somewhere. Search the back of drawers or cupboards and you'll find notebooks with beginnings but no middles or ends, pristine and abandoned along with the dream I had for a moment that I may actually write something worth reading. My *Stoner*. My *Folded Leaf*. My 'Jabberwocky'. Each story a fresh start and the best of intentions with promises of 'this time' only to be cast aside to make room for self-doubt and my waning confidence. This then followed by guilt and self-loathing for ideas above my station and who did I think I was anyway? But still it lives and rumbles, this desire or need to write, to make my mark. A niggling companion I fail to satisfy like an inevitability to make peace with and be remembered as the greatest writer that never was.

For somebody who has struggled with depression and their mental health, not to mention the tendency to catastrophise, the onset of a pandemic was a blow. Going into lockdown I, like the rest of the country, tried to keep calm and stagger on, eyeing with dread and a little curiosity this novel turn of events. I threw myself into cooking and video calls. I clapped for carers, wanting desperately to bask in the 'stronger together' glow. To make do and mend our sick nation. But as days, weeks, months passed, putting on my happy Zoom face became increasingly difficult. At best I was putting one foot in front of the other. At worst I was sat on the edge of the bed for hours, crying. Like the time I had run out of clean socks. It tipped me over the edge. Washing then rewashing my hands and showering relentlessly, holding my breath under my mask passing strangers because I was petrified, completely and utterly petrified of catching the virus.

Then it seemed we were getting through. Summer was here and we were coming back to life. Numbers were falling and I dared myself the luxury of hope. I was finding ways to cope. Music helped keep fear at arm's length for a few minutes and I did my best to stay low, keep brave. Panic attacks were less frequent and there was a tiny light at the end of what had been a long and dark tunnel. Then Autumn and with it fresh anxiety. The rollercoaster of tiers and school closures as numbers started to rise again. Headlines of redundancies, new strains and more deaths punctuated by the ping of notifications from a government app warning me that my number would soon be up.

The New Year arrived along with another lockdown as the virus spread with terrifying speed. I was in a constant, exhausting state of high alert, reluctant to leave the house because this lockdown was different, it was worse and I was struggling.

Then one day I received an email.

I have a friend called Amy. Amy is very special to me. She brightens my life just by being in it and at that moment I needed that light. Amy has a friend called Will. Will is an author and had spoken to Amy about his idea for a small writing group of, in his words, kind and open souls, to run for eight weeks and meet every Wednesday morning to play with their words, explore their writing, find their voices and share their stories. Terrified I said yes in the hope it would offer me a distraction and give me some confidence to, at the very least, put pen to paper. Will's friend Sonali said yes too and the four of us met for the first time the following week. Amy knew about my desire to write. What Amy didn't know was that the timing of her email was perfect. I needed something. I needed this and although I didn't know it, I needed to spend time with these people.

Our meetings soon became the anchor in my week. Will created a beautifully safe space, tethering me to something tangible that was calming my mind, comforting my soul. We completed writing activities Will referred to as games, him gently coaxing words out of us which we shared, shyly at first but with more confidence as the weeks went by. Tapping into memories of childhoods and holding each other's hands as our admiration for and connection to each other grew. I was writing and unbelievably my new writing family liked it. Writing about and revisiting experiences from my past meant I was beginning to have a greater understanding and sympathy for my relationship with my present. It was helping me cope.

I have always been afraid of judgment and just not being good enough. But I was learning, finding my style, hearing my voice. I was, and am, writing every day and have felt happier for it. Which is why I'm sharing these pieces with you, dear reader, along with notes about the activities and writing games that inspired them. Everything has a connection to a real memory even if chronologically speaking they may not have happened in the sequence you find here. But everything you read is real, deeply personal and I proudly include my coming out story in the hope it helps you know and understand me better.

This is just a beginning and I am excited about where my writing is taking me. I have been so worried and so anxious. But now I feel hopeful. Less worried and less anxious thanks to springtime and vaccines and friends and love. And writing. These short pieces will not change your life but they have changed mine. In fact, they very well may have saved it. And for that, dear friends, I am eternally grateful.

MY NAME IS JONATHAN

I was told it was a Hebrew word
　　　that means 'Gift from God'
and I always liked that so have never
　　　looked it up in case it's not true
and I'd be disappointed.

I was going to be called Stephan until my
　　　Dad told a workmate
who said it sounds like a girl's name and
　　　people would call me Steph

so, they decided to call me Jonathan and
I don't know if that is true but I like
        that story too.

I like my name.
I can feel my feet on the ground when
        I hear people say it out loud
and it still excites me when I see my name
because it's my name.

My Mum didn't let people call me Jon
but I've been called JD and Jonboy
        and Lala,
Mr Davies by hundreds of teenagers,
Fozzie, like the bear, by my Dad and
        sometimes Gravy Davies
because my middle name is Gray.

But, my name is Jonathan.

THE PAPER ROUND

I never got used to walking past the church at that hour, still dark in the winter, quickening my pace for a bit and not looking into the graveyard in case something moved, or didn't. Always relieved to turn the corner and deliver to The Semaphore Inn their Sun, peeking at Page 3 but lingering a little longer with the Page 7 Fella. The empty kegs from the night before giving off their faint beer fumes which I inhaled while taking in the glamour of the caravan park behind, lifeless now, and the bay beyond. The snow heavier, settling on the fur of Taffy's back and on the front of my scarf.

I turned towards the path at the foot of the Marion which we would roll down in Spring before the grass grew too long and land in a heap at the bottom, legs entwined, exciting me. A row of four houses ahead with a light on upstairs at Sunnyside, first signs of life. I walked up the path avoiding engine parts and bits of furniture which Auntie Rita would say was a disgrace. I lifted the flap and pushed the paper through carefully, trying not to make a sound, difficult because everything about this house was creaky, not wanting to disturb their dog and therefore the peace. Then three doors along to Sea View where Mrs Jones would sometimes be waiting for me with a sweet, most often a chocolate like the Milk Tray ones Grandma liked, wrapped in a tissue with a biscuit for Taffy. But not today and I left feeling disappointed because we looked forward to the treats. Mrs Jones was always dressed in black and had never married or had children and I was sad the morning I was a newspaper short because she had passed.

At Hill View I pressed my hands together in prayer because this is where Nain and Taid had lived and I was asking God to look after them, like I did every morning. I could see myself sitting on a little stool by the fire or on Taid's knees or with Nain in the kitchen wearing her pale blue overcoat cutting bread but Mum wasn't sure about that because Nain died when I was three and she doesn't think I can really remember. But I can and keep it to myself because I don't want to upset her. The outside toilet stands still at the end of the garden and I'm grateful I don't have to use one because Auntie Rita said that sometimes it was so cold she couldn't wee and we would laugh about it.

I deliver Mrs Venton's Daily Mail next door but one and I'm pleased because I didn't make any noise. All I could hear was the silent sound of snow falling.

Mrs Venton was Auntie Rita's bridesmaid and my godmother and Auntie Rita kept the wedding announcement from The Weekly News in one of her scrapbooks that said 'the bridesmaids wore white fur headdresses with matching muffs' which my sisters and I would read to each other until we were sick with laughing. Mrs Venton used to live above her shop which she turned into a living room after her husband died and she got too old to run it on her own. I would sometimes stop there on my way home from school and she gave me sweets but apart from that I didn't see her very often. She had kept the big shop window from where you could see all the way to Rhyl and Prestatyn and Uncle Pat would tell us he could see Blackpool Tower in England from there and we would spend ages looking for it. I hoped Mrs Venton didn't stand too close to the window in case a nuclear bomb was dropped on Liverpool and the blast shattered the glass, thinking it would be the city nearest to us that would be hit in a nuclear war because I wasn't sure the Russians had heard of Chester.

Everything was white, which it hadn't been when I set off. Mum had told me to wear the hat and scarf she had knitted because the sky looked full of snow and I was happy I listened to her. She would get up with me on those winter mornings because she didn't like the thought of me alone in the dark then went back to bed after I had left with two cups of tea. Grandma said I was losing my puppy fat and Mum would tell her it's because I walk miles every morning now and looked proud about that which made me happy. But she said that all that walking was stretching my legs and she couldn't let my trousers down anymore so I needed new ones and she looked proud about that too but pretended to be cross about it. I hoped we would get them from Boppers Boutique on Station Road and not from the indoor market which smelled of hamster hay.

I was still heading away from home towards the last house at the top of the hill where you waited for the bus to town. It was a bungalow where Stella Taylor, a girl in my class, lived. Her older brother, Wayne, had yellow hair and lots of freckles which the boys at school were mean about. I never told Stella that he would sometimes throw stones at me when he saw me coming and I would toss their Mirror over the gate and run then get into trouble because his mum would call Mr Lloyd and say the paper was wet. I also never told her about that time when we were little and playing Star Wars and Wayne said I had to show him my thing but I wouldn't. Sometimes he would stare at me in the playground at school and I didn't know why he looked so angry with me. Maybe it's because I wouldn't show him my thing.

There was a lane along the back of their bungalow where the Watsons lived and I was happy to reach it because it meant I was heading back in the direction of the estate. The snow was much heavier and Taffy looked like a sheep or an iced finger. I was sorry for him but happy for me that he was with me. Sometimes, if it was raining, Dad would take me in his car or come and get me and we would be finished in no time and I would go back to bed because it was still early. I prayed again for Dad to come and get us but God couldn't hear me this time and the snow squeaked under my feet.

At the end of the lane was the big house where the Monroes lived and I had to walk up their long drive to deliver their Times and it took me out of my way which sometimes annoyed me. Mum and Dad were friends with the Monroes because of the PTA and would be invited to cheese and wine evenings at their house which Mum would wear lipstick and her nice dress for. I liked Mr Monroe's happy face and Scottish accent and their teenage son, who always had his hands in his pants, said he fancied my sister which she said was disgusting but would smile about it at the same time. Mrs Monroe would sometimes be up and pour me some squash and make a fuss of Taffy. She gave me a selection box as a tip at Christmas but I wanted money really so I could spend it in Woolworths and I once said that to Mum

who said I was an ungrateful so and
so.

My knuckles and knees were cold so
I sang 'Do they know it's Christmas'
quietly to keep our spirits up and because I was practising the words to
sing along with Top of The Pops and
impress my sisters. By the time I got to
the Castle Inn at the back of the Marion, the snow was inches thick. I liked
it here because this is where Dad and
Uncle Pat would bring us for a drink
on Christmas Day while Mum and
Auntie Rita made Christmas lunch
and drank Snowballs and we would
sing carols all the way home. From
the Castle you could see Snowdon on
a clear day, but not today. I couldn't
even see Manchester House through

the snow at the top of the steep hill ahead of me which I was always glad to get to because it meant my bag would be nearly empty. Manchester House was tall and handsome and it scared me because children used to say that the lady who lived there had killed her husband because nobody ever saw him. But I had seen him leave early in the morning once and they said I couldn't have and that it must have been his ghost. The house was coming into view as I climbed the road and I reached in my bag for their Daily Post with 'M House' scribbled in the top right-hand corner of the front page, folded it then pushed it through the letterbox.

I was shivering and snowflakes were sticking to my eyelashes and I thought of Auntie Rita's friends at bingo who teased me saying it wasn't fair that a boy should have such nice long eyelashes and I would blush, which made them laugh. I couldn't see the road in front of me or the hill that should be on my left and felt a little panic that I might get lost in the snow and they would all be sad if Taffy came home without me. There was a crunch of footsteps coming towards me and I thought it was my imagination or the ghost from Manchester house until I heard Dad call my name. I was so happy to see him I started to cry and Taffy was too cold to wag his tail but I knew he would be happy too. Dad took my bag and put the blanket he kept in the car around me and we walked to the post office at the top of the road where he had left it in case it got stuck in the snow and we wouldn't be able to get back up.

I REMEMBER

I remember the arcade on Station Road near the Eateasy where we went for egg and chips with Auntie Rita and Uncle Pat.

I remember Auntie Rita putting coins in the slot machine with one hand and holding her cigarette with the other.

I remember the man who was always outside asking for change so he could buy cigarettes.

I remember boys laughing and throwing pennies at the ground and he picked them up until he had all the pennies and they had none.

I remember buying Superman sweet cigarettes and puffing on them and nibbling the ends so they got smaller and it looked like we were smoking.

I remember wanting to be older than I was.

I remember waiting for the bus outside the Imperial and the smell of stale beer and cigarettes.

I remember drinking pop through a straw and waiting for the balloon drop at the Four Oaks on Boxing Day.

I remember eating Findus French Bread Pizzas at Grandma's house.

I remember stealing a rubber from Woolworths.

I remember Auntie Rita putting a bunch of plastic grapes in the fruit bowl as a practical joke.

I remember my sister picking them up and then crying because we were all laughing.

I remember fighting with Darren Foster at the back of the coach home from swimming.

I remember sitting on the stairs listening to *War Of The Worlds* and thinking it was real.

I remember kicking my sister's Sindy House down the stairs.

I remember looking in the hallway mirror and cutting off my eyelashes because the boys said I looked like a girl.

I remember 518607.

I remember Holly the hamster coming back from the dead.

I remember 'tell your mum I saved your life'.

I remember daring each other to go into the graveyard on Halloween.

I remember being given headphones to wear all day to know how it felt to have a disability.

I remember wanting the blindfold or the crutches.

I remember going fishing with Dad and catching a chicken carcass.

I remember having a boxing match with David Brown in a ring the big kids made out of the hay bales.

I remember *Panorama* making me cry.

I remember our pond being frozen in August.

I remember.

THE PUPPY

Sunday lunches at 49 Gadlas Road were pretty much the same every week. There was the usual bickering with my sisters and one or two kicks under the table, ignoring mother's scolding of 'stop tantalising your brother' followed by sly side-eyed smiles and quick poking of tongues. Seated around the dining table for

six, could sit up to eight, in our new-
ly decorated home squeezed in by father's hifi stereo system and matching drinks cabinet, a perk from work
which didn't leave much room for anything else and was his pride and joy.
I had spent most of the morning and
Sunday lunch, begging my parents to
let us have a puppy, promising to walk
it, feed it and play with it, putting forward my case which, as usual, fell on
deaf ears. There followed the inevita-
ble discussion about going for a drive
which really meant trailing my parents around a garden centre and being
told not to drag my feet, only tolerated
by the promise of an ice cream from
Nino's on the way home. All I wanted
to do was disappear to my box room to
play records and flick through *Smash*

Hits magazines, trying to make sense of the flutters in my tummy I got from staring at pictures of Adam Ant or a bare-chested Sting. But there was to be no such escape. It was settled. We were going for a drive.

My older sister, Sian, Welsh for Jane, already edging herself away from family life due to her advanced years and not wanting to be seen in public with the rest of us, convinced mother that she had to stay and finish Mr Dewi Jones' English Literature homework. I could understand. An up close and personal with Mr Dewi Jones, his unsettling sidecomb, coffee breath and vicious streak was to be avoided at all costs. Nobody can hold their breath for that long. But I knew from the smirk on her lips as she got up from the table that she didn't have any homework and that she'd be straight on the phone to Arwel at number three within seconds of us leaving and they'd be on her bed French kissing to Culture Club, the thought of which made me feel a bit sick.

Excuses exhausted and defeat accepted, my little sister and I were bundled in the back of our father's sky blue Ford Cortina estate, his other pride and joy, and off we went. My forehead enjoyed the cool of the window as I barely registered the only too familiar route through Llandudno, Conway and Betws-y-Coed. All places I took for granted and whose beauty I would only appreciate thirty years later from

London, but that's a whole other story. The slate grey buildings were made blacker by the rain as we made our way through Snowdonia and along increasingly narrow roads, eventually turning into a farm yard and pulling up alongside one of the many outbuildings.

I was sulking. Before we left, I'd ran upstairs to put on the new, chocolate brown Farah trousers I had been bought, against mother's wishes, from Fosters menswear on a shopping trip to the Bay with Auntie Rita the day before. I was supposed to save them for church on Easter Sunday the following week but had not been able to wait and I was annoyed with myself, mostly, because I now wouldn't have anything new to wear and refused to get out of the car for fear of ruining them. Suit yourself was the general message and I watched as Mother, Father and my little sister walked away from the car and its moody prepubescent passenger through the now barely there rain shower, sparkling in the sun as it pushed its way through. A robust woman with a gammon pink complexion and matching tabard appeared from the main house and, after exchanging pleasantries, led them around the corner and out of my sight.

After not much time at all, my little sister came running back to the car breathless and excited, telling me that I really must come with her and that I really wouldn't regret it. I was curious, I admit, so reluctantly prised myself from the back seat and followed, watching where I was walking very carefully so as not to splash my trousers in a puddle or, worse, a fresh cow pat because then I wouldn't be able to wear them again, washed or not. As I came up behind the adults, my father turned and there in his arms was a golden ball of fur and it took me a moment to realise that he was holding a puppy and I could feel my eyes water and my chest lurch as my mother smiled and said 'this is Taffy and he belongs to us'.

SWIMMING POOL

1.

The dark outside made the glare from the lights even more cruel as they stood exposed by the side of the pool. Waiting for the instructor to place them with the partner they would have to save from drowning. He had never been in the leisure centre this late, his first adult class. His pale hairless, shapeless body betrayed his age despite attempts to stand a little taller and puff out his chest. He instinctively placed his hands in front of his Speedos, half in prayer, standing amongst the men with their broad shoulders and hairy chests willing himself not to make eye contact or take a sideways peek the way he would sometimes do in the changing room. There was a heavy woman at the end of the line he recognised but couldn't place and he tensed as she moved next to him and brushed a breast against him.

2.

Standing exposed by the pool they waited to be placed with the partner they would soon save from drowning. Excited to be in the leisure centre this late, his first adult class. His hairless body betraying his age despite best attempts to stand taller. Placing his hands in front of his Speedos, half in prayer, next to the broad-shouldered men with hairy chests not making eye contact or sneaking a peek like he would in the changing room. He recognised a heavy woman from somewhere and tensed as she stood next to him, brushing a breast against his arm.

3.

Standing exposed, they waited by the pool. Dark outside, his first adult class. Hairless next to the broad-shouldered bearded men. Willing himself not to look or catch their eye. Tensing when the heavy woman he would have to save stood next to him brushing him with her breast.

THE JUMP

Feeling desperate,
I sat with Carys at the Summit of the
      Marion behind school
while the others pointed and laughed
because I was too afraid to jump.

She gently rubbed my back
saying I didn't have to jump and
      she would sit with me

as long as I liked
or walk back down the way we
      had come from the village
and there would be no shame in it.

But there would be
nicknames and failures
and worse, nicknames linked to
      failures stuck
and we knew it.

So, I looked at her and she held
      my hand
I'll jump with you, she said
and I heard their cheers
and my heart leapt a few seconds
      behind the rest of me
and I don't remember anything
      after that.

THE RAILWAY STATION

We sit in the freezing cold, huddled together on Platform 1 waiting for the 13.55 to London Euston, avoiding meaningful conversation or anything controversial whilst sizing up the competition for a window seat. Busier than Platform 2 because nobody wants to go to Bangor. Not in February.

It's Sunday. We'd caught the bus to the station because Dad is the only one who can drive and he was in Ireland lugging his samples from shop to shop and staying in B&B's. Mum says he likes it really because he enjoys a full English. We make small talk. Politely discussing I don't remember what because the elephant that has been in the room all week is now sat between us and I'm burning to tell her and, unknown to me, she's longing for me to spit it out, put us both out of our misery.

The station is bigger than necessary, I think. The elaborate Victoriana harking back to heydays, now past its prime like the matching pier you can see from the end of the platform selling rock, pop and the world's smallest bibles, to nobody.

New arrivals try the locked waiting room door in vain and we smirk. If they looked, they would see the absence of glass in the windows that give no protection from the icy winds blowing in from the North Sea. She pulls her coat tighter around her neck and I reminisce out loud about times I have sat here waiting for school trips to start and teenage adventures to unfold after reaching the border. This place I had waited years to leave, but come back to time and again until I run out of reasons to. Running along this Platform to get a final look of Sian returning to University. Her visits shorter and more infrequent by her final year. Crying on the platform when my turn came and pressing my damp face against the window as the train pulled away to see my family for as long as I could as they trotted beside the carriage waving their goodbyes, then running out of platform and my sight.

We laugh about the time we caught the train to Chester to buy ski jackets from C&A because that was the fashion. Dad asking why we needed them when we had perfectly good donkey jackets from the army surplus and besides, we'd never be able to afford to go skiing. Needing the toilet and jumping off at Rhyl running as fast as I could while Mum stood half on, half off the train so it couldn't leave without me, laughing and shouting 'brysiwch brysiwch' as the conductor screamed at her to get back on, or off.

I look over at the always shut kiosk for something to do with my eyes and pluck at the flaking red paint on the bench, scratching for the courage to tell her what it was I had come home for knowing we would be alone for the week, but sit there still petrified and burdened. I feel lightheaded, sick, achy with intention to say those two small words that would change our lives forever. Standing and pacing, then sitting again. On repeat.

'People are going to think you've got ants in your pants love' she says looking me in the eye, patient.

Choosing *Philadelphia* on VHS from the newsagent opposite where, years earlier, Tanya Parry and I had failed to convince Mrs Jones that Dad wanted to rent *The Evil Dead* to watch that afternoon then losing our nerve and running out laughing and empty handed – 'If your Dad wants to watch *The Evil Dead*, Jonathan Davies, he will have to come and collect it himself'.

I watched her more than I did the film, assessing her reaction, reading into each eyebrow twitch, faint smile or tiny frown. Relieved to see her upset when Tom Hanks died which I thought was a good sign. Her hands resting in her lap, thumbs spinning around each other as she always does when she is thinking, which we would notice and copy to be cheeky.

A day trip to Manchester where we had tea cakes at John Lewis. Little squares of butter melting on them while I told her about my friend Adrian who had a boyfriend. Then walking her up and down Canal Street, arm in arm, pointing at two bearded men holding hands to make sure she saw them and could say that it was disgusting and look away which she didn't and I thought that was a good sign too. But they had seen me point and looked hurt or angry or both and I was sad all the way home because I couldn't go back and tell them that I was sorry and had needed their help.

The train appears and we rise as one, gathering bags and preparing to depart from this life and dive head first into the other. I repeat the words over and over, screaming them silently in my head, refusing to leave my mouth. My useless, cowardly, deceitful mouth that has kissed boys and told others, but not her. This mouth that has got me into trouble for saying too much like when Carys and I were busy talking in Further Mathematics and Mr Jacks threw a board duster at us, hitting me on the head and I nearly cried but held it in because I would have never been allowed to forget it.

I walk towards the edge promising God that I would write and tell her. That I'm happy and she shouldn't worry. That I'd left because I needed to and that I'd been to places where there were others like me, lots of them and I had found my people, my story, my home. I'd tell her I'm sorry. Sorry I hadn't told her first. Sorry if I'd let her down. Sorry I wouldn't give her grandchildren or get married and that she would always be the most important woman in my life, hoping she would like that. I'd ask her to forgive me and not disown me and tell her I hoped she still loved me and that I'm scared but am the same person she had linked arms with on Station road, proudly introducing me to people who had known me all my life, telling them that I lived in London, making it her achievement too. Which it is. It all is.

The train pulls up along the platform. Holding each other one last time before I board, failed in my mission, mentally hitting the sides of my head with my fists and our imagined future, where we whisper in the kitchen about the man I'd brought home to meet her, was in the pit of my stomach. I throw my bag on a seat and return to the door where she is still standing and lower the window, reaching out my hands to meet hers like we always do. She looks up at me through watery eyes, holds my fingers tightly and says 'I know, I think I've always known and I love you very much. I always have and I always will. Call me when you get back love and don't worry, I'll sort it all out with your father.'

Auntie Rita holding me outside my first home, 11 Bodryfedd Terrace in Llysfaen

Me on Mum's knee at my first birthday party in Auntie Rita and Uncle Pat's back yard in Colwyn Bay

My christening at St Cynfran's Church in Llysfaen
L to R: Mrs Venton, Mr Venton, Mum, Dad, Nain, Sian, Taid, Auntie Rita, Uncle Pat

Auntie Rita and Mum

Emma's christening at St Cynfran's Church in Llysfaen

Dad, Sian and me outside 11 Bodryfedd Terrace

Emma and me in the back garden of 49 Gadlas Road in Llysfaen

NOTES

MY NAME IS JONATHAN

This was a lovely exercise or 'writing game' as Will would call them. We were given four minutes to write about our name. We were asked to think about what our names mean to us, other names we have been called, nicknames and how our name makes us feel. He gave us the starter sentence and we took it from there. This is exactly what I wrote in those four minutes, unedited. These 'games' were so important, not only to encourage us to write but to focus our minds and put to one side whatever stress or worries we brought to the sessions with us. So, we would clear our minds, take a few deep breaths and begin, not only freeing our creativity but allowing us a few meditative moments away from the pressures of our outside worlds.

THE PAPER ROUND

A few weeks into knowing each other it was interesting to observe the ways in which our discussions and observations about each other's writing started to evolve. It is a privilege to listen to somebody read something they have created a few moments ago and we were beginning to learn things about each other we hadn't shared much before, if at all. That's exactly what writing together was doing, it was opening us up to each other in a safe place without judgement and therefore fear. It was wonderful to me that this was all happening on Zoom and I had only met one of these people I was now spending every Wednesday morning with before. I often wondered what the experience would have been like if we met each week in the real world and whether or not we would have been as open and as brave about sharing so much.

Around halfway through our time together, Will asked us to think about one of our first jobs. Most of the time I would think of something straightaway and feel sure about it but as the nine minutes we were given started, I still wasn't certain where to start. I'd had a number of part time jobs as a teenager (someone had to fund my vinyl obsession) but as my paper round at age eleven was my first I decided to go with that. I did not know where to begin, but as I closed my eyes and imagined the route I took every morning, I pictured the Church in the dark and how it made me feel and I had my first sentence. The first paragraph you see here is what I wrote in the session and feeling encouraged by the others, decided to spend some more time with it and shared this extended draft a couple of weeks later. I liked how the paper round gave me a structure to work from, allowing me glimpses into people's lives simply by delivering their papers every morning. The stories are mostly true with a few additions taken from other experiences but I like that it has a start, a middle and an end. I can still remember the relief I felt when my father would appear on those cold winter mornings.

I REMEMBER

To encourage us to write between sessions, Will would email us some thoughts and ideas for us to think about and if we wished to, write about. One email included an introduction to the American artist Joe Brainard who, in 1970, published his first volume of autobiography called *I Remember*. Will described it as a series of short paragraphs (some just one sentence long) beginning with the words 'I remember' telling us that various writers have played around with the form and pointed us to 'I Ran All the Way Home' by the poet Paul Farley from his collection *Tramp in Flames* which I subsequently read and loved. Will suggested that we think about a place or period of time, a subject or an idea and write our own 'I remember' story. One of the many surprising but fantastic things about our sessions together were the places in my past they transported me to and my 'I remember' attempt took me back to the amusement arcades and shopping streets of my youth in North Wales. I can't explain why and that was part of the excitement, you didn't know where your mind or writing was going to take you next. So, this is my 'I remember' story, only draft and unedited and it really is a wonderful way to get you writing. As Will told us, 'borrow from the form and do what you like with it' encouraging us to be free and make it our own.

THE JUMP

This was a challenging but brilliant writing game. We each had to choose a random letter from the alphabet until we had seven. We then had to start to write, but the first seven words had to begin with one of the chosen letters in the sequence in which they were originally selected and we were given four minutes to write. It really focused the mind and at first was difficult but a name came to me beginning with the 'C' and that instantly took me to a place and experience from my childhood and the rest grew from there. I was and still am pleased with the result you see here. We then did the exercise again with seven new letters but I struggled and what I eventually wrote felt forced because it was. I felt frustrated but learnt that writing doesn't always come easily and not to let that discourage you or give up and that the important thing is to try again and keep writing.

THE PUPPY

This piece of writing was the first we wrote together. We were nervous, not knowing what to expect and after introductions and polite greetings Will asked us to close our eyes and think back to when we were ten years old. He asked us to remember the tastes and smells of being ten, the things around us and what they felt like to the touch. We wrote short notes and shared our memories which were heartfelt and loving. I was struck by how willing we all were to open ourselves up to each other so quickly and how lovely that was. I felt instantly safe in their company. Will then asked us to think about an experience that involved the first encounter with an animal. It could be any animal from any point in our lives with the only stipulations being that the animal appears at the end of the piece and it must finish with a sentence of dialogue. I revisited the piece a few times after the session and here you'll find the version I've spent time with and edited, drawing on memories of growing up in our semi-detached house in Llysfaen, North Wales which as you can see became a time I was regularly and happily drawn back to as the weeks went by.

SWIMMING POOL

This may at first seem like an odd piece to include but I loved this as an exercise and as an appreciation of the power of editing. I learnt that it takes real confidence to take words away and that sometimes more is said by what isn't included than by what is. I think this is a nice example of that. We discussed at great length that at times it is important to let the reader fill in the gaps themselves with things taken from their own experiences, drawing them in and therefore becoming more invested in the writing. We were asked to think about a time when we were swimming. It could be anywhere from indoor or outdoor pools, a river or the sea, at any point in our lives. Unsurprisingly, I found myself right back in North Wales, this time as a teenager attending my first lifesaving class for adults at the local Colwyn Bay Leisure Centre. We were given seven minutes but could not write more than one hundred and fifty words. We were then given a few minutes to write the piece again but in only a hundred words then finally, once more in only fifty words. I loved listening to everybody's pieces and how they transformed. It was fascinating to see what was excluded and which parts survived. Editing your work is not easy but I like to think that where I ended up is a good example that sometimes less can be more.

THE RAILWAY STATION

It was our second session together and we had just completed the 'My name is...' game when Will asked us to pick a number. Each number corresponded to a place such as a café, gym or hair salon. We were then asked to think about the place and write about it for four minutes. My number, seven, meant my allocated place to write about was a railway station. My mind immediately took me to Colwyn Bay station as it had played an important role in my life which may sound like an odd thing to say about a railway station but having read the piece I hope you can appreciate why. I'm not sure Will had imagined that a railway station would be where one of the most defining moments of my story so far took place. As we were only given a short amount of time, I could only hint at this but when Will asked us to work on something to share in our final session I had an overwhelming desire to finish what I started and returned to the railway station. Of all the pieces it is the one that is the most intensely personal and the writing I am most proud of. I put parts in, then took them out again, as my confidence about sharing this moment came and went and although it's far from perfect, it is inherently me. When our last session came around, far too quickly, the nerves I had felt before our first returned. I just didn't know what reaction to expect. After hearing the beautiful pieces Amy and Sonali had written, I took a deep breath and began, glad not to have to see their faces when I stumbled in places as the feelings from the moment resurfaced and I became very emotional. I finished and there was silence but when I raised my head to look at the screen I saw that they were all, like me, crying. It is a moment I will never forget nor will I the love, friendship and support I was shown by this group that were once mostly strangers.

ACKNOWLEDGMENTS

This little book is, in its way, a big thank you to Amy Gadney, Sonali Wijeyaratne and William Fiennes because without them I wouldn't have found my voice or the confidence to share it.

Thank you to everyone who has encouraged, commented, liked, posted, direct messaged and donated. And thank you to those who have listened on dog walks and over cups of tea. Celebrated with me in the kitchen or made me laugh in the pub. Let me talk or have a cry when I was finding it hard to cope. I have been overwhelmed with your love, friendship and support.

Thank you Todd Swift and everyone at BSPG for believing in my little book and for your care.

Thank you to my family for being proud and patient and for letting me share our stories. You are simply the best.

And Josh. I love you.

Most of all, thank you for picking up this little book and for receiving it in the way in which it is intended. And that is, with love.